TREMORS

Also by Cammy Thomas

Cathedral of Wish

Inscriptions

TREMORS

Cammy Thomas

Four Way Books
Tribeca

for my sister, Dorothy Q. Thomas, with love and gratitude

Library of Congress Cataloging-in-Publication Data

Names: Thomas, Cammy, author.
Title: Tremors / Cammy Thomas.
Description: New York : Four Way Books, [2021] |
Identifiers: LCCN 2021005288 | ISBN 9781945588938 (paperback)
Subjects: LCGFT: Poetry.
Classification: LCC PS3620.H626 T74 2021 | DDC 811/.6--dc23
LC record available at https://lccn.loc.gov/2021005288

This book is manufactured in the United States of America and printed on
acid-free paper.

Four Way Books is a not-for-profit literary press. We are grateful for the assistance
we receive from individual donors, public arts agencies, and private foundations.

This publication is made possible with public funds from the
National Endowment for the Arts

and from the New York State Council on the Arts, a state agency,

We are a proud member of the Community of Literary Magazines and Presses.

Contents

I.

II.

III.

I.

Mum

out in the world
our smiles look perfect
inside the house
dread keeps us mum

our smiles look perfect
the driveway is long
dread keeps us mum
no one can hear

the driveway is long
his braided horsewhip
no one can hear
old leather frayed

his braided horsewhip
we laugh at him
old leather frayed
under the table

we laugh at him
he grabs our legs
under the table
pulled out kicking

he grabs our legs
his ten year old girl
pulled out kicking
points the shotgun

his ten year old girl
no one can hear
points the shotgun
dread keeps us mum

The Eye of the Malign

The eye of the malign is a cold blue eye
                    that stares from the heart of every scene

It laughs when you cry and cries when you laugh
                    like no other eye that's ever been

The symmetries of evil, little sport and big,
                    flash on the eye's cold screen

If you let it in to where you live
                    it will burn a hole without being seen

Sometimes it looks out from the waist of a dress
                    on a woman in the dust

Or it's on a ship too long at sea
                    where the decking has turned to rust

Babies see it when they wake at night
                    if strangers come to their cries

Horses patient in a dusky field
                    run off if it's in the sunrise

Which way you turn doesn't matter in the end—
                          the eye of the malign is there

Its saving grace, if grace there is,
                          is that its gaze goes everywhere

The Thing from Another World

My brother kept a sword by his bed
after he saw *The Thing from Another World*,
a huge humanoid space creature
frozen under the ice.

Thawed by Arctic scientists,
the creature broke out of the lab,
tried to kill everyone.

Jim said a man could crawl
into our bedroom from the porch roof,
so he lay awake in the next bed
ready to draw his sword.

The creature had swiped a paw off a husky—
under bright lights, the paw twisted, scraped.

One night, woken by a noise,
Jim pulled his sword from the scabbard,
snuck into the hall.

Lost in the dark, determined to save us,
he turned, something rising in his throat,
a piercing animal scream.

Our father appeared in the dark—
"What are you," he said, "a scared little girl?"

But Jim knew the creature was still there,
clung to his heavy sword—
it wasn't easy, frozen under the ice.

Neighbors

During winter, the Swedes next door
made a sauna with hot rocks and a tent.

We would sweat, then run out,
flinging ourselves in the snow

while the grownups downed shots
of aquavit and fought. In blizzards,

they'd hitch up their black horse, Brandy,
ski behind him down drifted streets.

Once, our mother drove over to pick us up,
saw their mother and our father naked

in the lit bathroom window,
turned the big Chevy around.

Their bomb shelter had food and space
for their family only. Their daughter Christina

said they kept a loaded shotgun by the door.
If we tried to get in, sadly, they'd have to shoot us.

After their dad left, Christina used to open
the garage door, turn off the car,

and, swearing in Swedish, drag her mom out
onto the lawn. Then call 911

while her mom lay there turning blue.

Wildfire

My brother set fire to a field
my sister and I were sitting in—
first smoke, then spreading flames.

I saw the smoke, pulled her
to her feet, started to run.
She was little, slow.

Just as I decided to aim for the woods
the trucks came. We ran
around the burning circle.

They sprayed floods on the hay
until the field was bare, smoldering.
When we reached the house,

the men were looking for hot spots.
My sister's face was red. My father
yanked my brother's arm,

shoved the side of his head as he sat
on an old stump, staring
at his blackened fingertips.

Rocketgirl

I frayed
my mother's temper
ran around
disobeyed
saw myself a
glorious boy tall
wild and mild
sometimes had to be
shoved
into a dress
cried pitifully

featherless robin
fallen I made
a cotton nest
in the bathroom sink
tried to feed it worms
but in the night
it vanished
maybe the cat
I was stoic

forbidden inside
on summer days

ran down green roads
to Lilac Land
sweet perfume
purple and white
made me dizzy
lost on winding paths
waving a wooden sword
locked my mother
in tangled branches
made her beg
to be let out

Our Father

he made a play
we went to see
and like a play
it saw us too

he made us stand
recite our lines
until we saw
no way to stop

we told each other
of the myth
he built for us
of blood and stone

our thoughts were not
our own
we shivered under
heavy manes

like horses running
from a blast
the stars the stars
fast slid away

took their noise
to other skies
left us here
without the play

how could it
be otherwise

Fairy Tale

peerless father drops
his twins aged ten
in foreign woods
rundown cabin

animals scratching
in the walls
one drafty bed
side by side

play in leaf litter
eat what he left them
hot August sky
sun creeps up

boy climbs the ladder
dim attic torn paper
hairless baby mice
pink paws like needles

girl walks tearless
jumps to a hawk scream
slither in leaves
down an animal trail

can't see the stars
dead-leaf driveway
watch in the dust
three days then four

shoulder their hunger
hide in the cabin
comes their father
strange woman beside him

French Toast

ah my mother used to make it
with eggs and milk
and stale white bread

slid onto a plate with
Log Cabin fake maple syrup
and I always wanted more

to disappear what troubled me
the man under the moon
the man in our living room

make enough spitting bacon
to forget the broken game boards
splintered bat

missing family car
his vanishings and sudden returns
smelling of other rooms

my mother's tears
over the stove
her catchy milky breath

Lamentation to Our Lord

It was wrong that my mother tried and tried and
tried and always failed.
When she insisted she didn't believe, You could have extended mercy.
Surely You saw her mind, susceptible,
twist, yearn—
her lone consolation the ice clink in her glass?

You could have helped her stop hearing it.
You could, at least, have tamed her unspeakable mother,
or maybe knocked off that ghastly husband
in some unaccountable accident.
Or why not go all the way, since You could—
translate her, like St. Catherine,
to the slopes of Mount Sinai—
let doves break forth from her blissful heart?

She could not put the glass down.
"I don't know them," she said at last of her children,
"but I know I love them."
Are You listening? Are You?
Why spin her like a circus bear
tethered before the crowd?

Possessed

Long Island Sound had red tides
but we didn't care,
swam anyway.

I was always hungry
for rare burgers at the beach club,
a pile of buttery rice,

high-water diving board.
We had a Rolls at one point,
got sand in it,

bumped across the wood bridge
over the swamp
bouncing on British springs.

Of course it got repossessed.
We loved the hymns in church,
crooned like wild wolves,

hair uncombed, hungry eyes,
dressed all cockeyed,
clink of beach rocks under our feet.

Ivy grew through the screens.
Dad boffed the lady next door, while
Mom played cowboy songs on her guitar,

"poor wrangler Joe" and
"see them tumbling down."
Bees stung in the lawn.

"The Blues in My Heart, the Rhythm in My Soul"
—*for SMM*

Sally asked for my Elmore James album—
the only time she asked me for anything
in the eight years she cooked
and cleaned and washed our hair,
picked us up from school,
helped us bathe and choose our clothes.

She had two kids of her own near Mobile,
older kids she rarely saw. She hated
Long Island cold. Her friends
from the Black beauty salon
sometimes came over and talked
in her basement room.

One night when I was about fourteen,
they told me I should color my hair,
put highlights in, pluck my shaggy
brows. They smiled at me, but
after I left the room, a burst of giggles.

Once, our old dog had a seizure
in the kitchen, flipped over
foaming at the mouth, and Sally
ran out—grabbing me on the way—

slammed the kitchen door,
fled to her room. Rescued,
I sat on the living room floor
while the dog howled.

I liked that album a lot,
and her asking for it made me
like it more. I told her no.

II.

White and Black in the Suburbs

—for CK and SG

At lunch I say,
"After I washed the pants five times
they streaked,
so I took them back—
no receipt—and they
gave me new ones."

The two women look at their food.
"That would never happen
to me. Never," Sherry says,
and Claudia: "Without a receipt—no."

Out on the street,
my car has a ticket,
theirs not. "On the other hand,"
Claudia says, "we've got
the parking thing down."

We laugh—
a laugh like a rusty gate,
like a hacksaw.

Chilling Kills

I'm a killer
from my living room
among my lovely things

a killer swimming
in a cool pool
trying not to hurt anyone

under my own
tall trees a killer
everything about me

kills even in my everyday
shoes even in
my cool pool

in my living room
I take it as a given
nothing wicked comes

mowers mowing
I vacuum dust away
while somehow killing

I take it as a given
how clean we keep it
how wicked

these chilling kills
of people I don't see
because I'm vacuuming

how clean we keep it
my America
how free of weeds

Nothing Touches Me

for ten years she's been working
a needlepoint pillow
of her husband's family crest
three ravens in profile beaks open
and motto *Nothing Touches Me*

today she left it in a cab
they were late
her sister-in-law rushing
so rude to the taxi man
it was under her old pink coat
already she's called Manhattan Taxi
Lost and Found three times
everyone says she's become forgetful

done except the gold border
glossy ravens gloating in boxes three
motto in red so right
when he said to her *forget it*
you can start again
his words burned in the air
she longed to stab him
with her hooked needle

she remembers finding the right pillow
then the light brown background
that took six years

she's seen ravens
pick at a dead dog in the road
plumage unspoiled
black heads glistening
handsome birds
glossy in the rain
ready for blood

Lattice

She's a lattice,
can't close back up.

The part where her head was—
it's a crisscross.

Now she holds
thorny climbing roses

that hide the violence they do,
her fractured frame softening,

warping till it snaps
under nodding flowers,

six heads to a stem.
Bearing them, she remembers

life as a tree,
when she could look down

and see a body entire,
no strange growths splitting her

with their exploded meanings.

Orbiting

Orbiting above the earth, watching
it loop by in its interstellar
loneliness, caught in my spacesuit,
air running out, can't stop the wobble—
I wake in my spaceship, under layers
of quilts. Still dark outside,
and in this cocoon waiting, thin air
full of doubt, I turn and see
out the porthole of my eye
a form like a far-off mountain range
moving slightly, rising and falling,
and I shift toward it until my ship
docks gently against my husband's body.

The Box

She arrived ahead of schedule
so they put her in a plastic box.
Not quite three pounds,
froggy legs curled under her.

I could stand pediatric
intensive care for an hour at most.
One confident mother
held her tiny son,
stayed all day to bathe
his inch-long feet
after the docs
pricked his heels for blood.
He was too small to scream.

Once a boy all yellow,
too sick for the box,
splayed out, paralyzed,
on a warming table,
chest heaving from a breathing
machine. They covered him
with bubble wrap as
he had no heat of his own.

His mom and dad came
with a priest, nurses
pulled the privacy screen,
and we all heard baptism—
then last rites. Next day,
he was gone. "Don't worry,"
the resident told us, "we'll tell you
if your baby's dying."

We decided to name her
Claire. When we bent
to the hole in the box,
and softly called her name,
her breathing faltered.

This Moving Ship Our Life

I said I love you darling when Claire left
with ancient suitcase, duffel full of shoes,
left for a new life she could not yet see.

I advised her where to walk, where not—
which side of the street can save your life—
and to be correct with everyone at work,

even those she comes to deeply hate.
She nodded patiently, swung one leg
over the other, tucked her heavy hair

behind her ears and watched the ticket window
as we waited for the train. She leaned her head
on my arm—where else could she have gone,

where else could I? Was there another way
to walk back to my car without imagining
the unspeakable things that happen every day?

When someone sat down next to her,
would she pretend to read, or fall asleep,
head inclining toward some other shoulder?

New Apartment

Oh, it was such a mess when Emma moved in with him,
clothes on every surface, walls still unpainted,

food mixed with mail, boxes on the steel table—
them kissing under the moonlight despite the rent,

despite his allergic cough, despite not knowing when
their last cries would fade in the heavy wind.

They hung his moon landing photos on the walls,
feeling maybe a waxing gibbous moon of love,

finding something of each other in themselves
next to the house-high stack of laundry.

I watched them closing in on something ineffable,
removable. How hard to look for their connection

and watch myself miss it, sliding by later—even while
my grown girl still crawls into my lap sometimes.

Wrapping Up

When we packed their kitchen
just before she and he moved to L.A.,
I double-wrapped everything:
a layer of foam, then newsprint.
A mother does not want to break anything.
We filled boxes with wedding presents:
cake slicers, nesting bowls, her new dishes
still in their cardboard cases,
white with thin gold rims,
a pattern her great grandmother
would have loved. All her dreams in them,
something to give her children
should they appear. Gold and white,
good fortune and purity—but death, too.

I wish for her the permanence
she has fought for. We packed the glass
vases, so delicate, packed
the commemorative mugs: her college,
Christmas, the hearts and arrows
of her high school love grown
into something tough and fragile.
He wasn't there that day, out saying goodbye

to his oldest friend, left her
with me, wrapping things up
in their rented kitchen.

Widow

her calves solid slabs above men's orthopedic shoes

100 blocks of Manhattan she marched in every weather

through Harlem down to the Village five miles daily

wearing her long-dead husband's warm long underwear

every kind of person picked her up if she fell

bent over at ninety-six still walking she could barely see

when icy snow made the sidewalk a treachery

upright joyous alone she went out feeling her way

around the block touching the buildings' cold stone

Trip to the Sound

All roads new to our mother,
roads she'd driven for fifty years.

"Has that always been there?
Slow down, let me see!"

Late fall, low sun, last leaves
still clinging, we took her

to the beach at low tide.
Head slipping forward, she snored.

Leaving her in the car we crossed
the footbridge onto cool sand.

She was finding vodka somewhere,
my sister and I agreed, dipping our feet

in the fish-stink of Long Island Sound.
Search her apartment again?

She slept comfortably, head on chest,
clutching her mother's old black purse.

Fish Gods

Praying to the sea for a sign
    that she wouldn't die for a while,
        Cynthia leaned on the rails staring at the fish
  as they rasped their teeth on coral
that can tear ships to shreds.

  Her blonde head turned side to side along the horizon
        while her shocked insides churned and multiplied.
Glowing fish swam in schools,
    reflecting and staring unharmed,
        magnified by the oily waves.

Winter Bonnets

   —after Rilke's "Fifth Duino Elegy"

where are those holy wanderers

their healing herbs
their ornately flowing inscriptions

what crushed them
those fiercely blossoming roses

their gaping faces their thin surfaces
savagely wrung out

how can we live on without them
their bright red knowing

how quiet our still small griefs
in spring summer autumn

blindly creating
our usual fallen unripe fruits

why this heavy wind
suddenly this laborious nowhere

forever saved up forever hidden
how can we make them return

snug in their winter bonnets

The Chain

Dorothy turned her hat
in her dark fingers. I sipped.

"Or when Grandma marched
with the suffragettes in London.

The point is, we're all activists.
The women, anyway." she said.

I thought of our mother,
chained to her round of duty,

unable to leap free no matter
how shattering the attempt.

"If I had the money, I'd rent a studio."
She glared greenly at me. I suggested

she write while the kids were in school.
"But the dog," she said, "the house,

always some repairman coming
and me the only one home."

Force

the leaves hid everything. I was very young
*

the muscular strength of men until someone
*

which I try not to think about
*

I found dead wasps beneath the nest, their pale
*

it was fifty years ago and I can't remember
*

forced me down, pulled a knife. He
*

after heavy rain last weekend, the nest
*

tears, sweat dropping in the dirt while
*

heads bowed, thick antennae slicked back
*

took me into the woods. I hadn't realized
*

paper wasps built an enormous nest
*

hands like hot wrenches. Should I have
*

someone had held my sister down, too

*

made of spit and leaves, buzzing

*

must have done it before—he knew

*

the wasps have gone, leaving only their dead

*

his face. I told myself no man would ever

*

Great White

When my sister and her lover
told my father they were marrying,
he slammed his fist on the placemat,
shouted, "That's ridiculous,"
and left the table.

She and her husband
warned weekend guests,
"Don't go to the pool,
don't look at the pool
until after 7 a.m."

Daily at dawn, uninvited,
my father drove to my sister's
in his bathrobe, walked to the pool,
dropped the robe, dove in naked,
crawled for a few minutes,

slapping the water,
flipped over, torso pale, bulky
under reflecting sky, floated
in the deep end staring
at the trees, at the windows.

After his swim he'd
climb out, pull on his robe,
leave. Never spoke to anyone.
Sometimes he'd raise a hand
to whoever was in the kitchen.

My Father's Bathrobe

for summer blue and white seersucker
> *my sister froze when she saw me in it*

I took it when he died and I've washed it
> *because of how he liked to slam us around*

a thousand times it's ankle-length and almost like
> *how he used to spend his time lying to us mocking*

women's clothes the arms not too long for me
> *why was I wearing it couldn't I feel the poison*

sometimes I garden in it because it's cool and
> *how could I put it on as if it made me sentimental*

because I know he used to care about such things
> *about him destroying our lives I must be deluded*

he was a crazy motherfucker but I have changed
> *the damage he would do the cruelty*

I have made the bathrobe something good that's all my own

August, Race Point Beach, Provincetown

We walk the shell-less shore
                    looking for a gentle slope in.
          Warm breeze, cold water.
Two large seals cruise parallel to the beach
                    and I think of sharks. We go in fast,
          out faster, seaweed on our backs.
The seals vanish. Two young men
                    cross the dunes, strip, submerge, stroll off.
                              Whale boat on the horizon, no spouts.
          Round blue sky, half-moon.

We walk companionably,
                    noticing each other's bodies.
          Today, my hip isn't aching,
                    the bugs aren't biting him.
Down the beach, two currents meet
          uneasily on a sandbar,
                    rippling in an extended line.
          Thirty-three years with almost no fighting.
He hands me a skipping stone.

Forty Years On

I love how you disobey me,
loose, muscular bodies draped
around the room. Whatever
I want you to do, your heads drop down
during Homer, Tennyson.

A boy might bury himself, pale,
brilliant behind dirty red
hair, might say nothing
despite every trick I know.
Or you, girl, bringing up Wittgenstein,
knowing no one knows who the fuck
that is. You're baiting me—
will I put you in your place?

You all rush, whispering like a river,
tremble like marble turning
to leaves, your golden hair,
your brown hair, top-knotted,
or brushing the backs of your chairs,
your crowded loneliness.

You ask: can't a soul ever change?
Eternal deities, all forthcoming,

you climb twined trellises
into sunburnt mirth. I used to think
I was there with you—was I there
with you?

        In the middle of *Macbeth*,
look at the arm I hold out to you,
its surprising, papery skin, its ropy veins.

I'm your grandmother now—
your liquid animal eyes look at me
as down a long tunnel,
across a galaxy.

III.

Three White Horses

I forgot where we were
meeting tonight—
actually, I forgot
we were meeting at all
until you called.

I forgot your mother
had died. Or I knew
someone's mother had.
Had you told me her story?
Was she the one
whose older sister
was a suicide?
Did she beat you,
or am I thinking
of someone else?

Coming to your house again,
I feel I've never been here.
How could I misplace
that bright green wall,
this windy road, the field
with three white horses?

Ladder

six rungs above the ground
night in heavy rain eager

to pull a clot of leaves
from a blocked downspout

sopped blinded
on my sixty-eighth birthday

in my old nightgown
slick aluminum ladder

climbing to the downspout
midair in the drench

my feet slipped off—
I went flying

caught myself gasp
slammed flat against

the flexing rungs
gutter cascading

spout still blocked
backed down

took the shining ladder
back to the garage

Dream of Two Dark Dresses

two dark dresses
are all that hang
in my closet
I don't want to wear
either of them

one is woven with
a scene of desolation
everything broken
no one has tools
the ones in charge are liars
the fabric sags
its blacks slack
and wet as oil

the other dress is fear
dark without a color
you can't move much
when you wear it
death seems so close
skirts like a cloud
of strangers' exhalations

wake up wake up
pick something else

Tremors

—for Gabrielle Calvocoressi

Provincetown Harbor is on the other side of the houses
               past the tall linden on Pearl Street
         kshhhh kshh of vibrating leaves

               next to a purple house
a small girl with a pinwheel is crying

         when the wind comes the boats all face right
which way is east

                    sometimes I don't care whether things matter
to anyone but me

         the pink roses don't care either
they grow for someone else's pleasure
                    but they don't know it

the girl's mother is so mad
               stop running in the street
         she grabs her roughly—too roughly

                    weedy oyster-shell driveway
               partial view of the unreachable
bay—dark pink hollyhocks—tremor in my hand makes writing hard

hhhhhhh in the leaves

      the father untangles the girl
    from her red-faced mother
leads her down the street still carrying her pinwheel

a pile of clamshells in the driveway

    I'm drowning

the mother has vanished

     we can never walk back the spent
        peonies keep their green but their faces
are spikes now

Except For

I keep thinking about
my estranged other brother—
his fruit-choked garden,
rock shoulders, clear eyes—
even when he whispered
I'd better watch my back—
about how, except for my fear,
I would love to see him again.

Off the Job

just wanted to say
I don't boss anymore

keeping kids safe
is so yesterday

no more birds
forbidden to fly

or fences containing
whatever goodbye

my stop-that voice
is out of gas

done crushing
done buckling up

now I'll
be the wild

blame my bad behavior
on the lion's breath

hot growl in the grass
my sizzling ass

Leaving Massachusetts

What about Santa Barbara?
We consider a house with a "cocktail pool"
in which an inflated dinosaur glides,
teardrop-tiny for a tiny yard.
Small house, cracked cement walks,
hint of a view—a zillion dollars.

But there'd be dolphins in the water,
breeze through twisty live oaks,
tamales with extra tang,
limitless sky, mountain backdrop.
A person could breathe.

How move to a smaller house
when I can't even jettison my aunt's slides
of trips in the 60s to Kuala Lumpur?
I gave the projector away,
dumped some carousels on my brother,
but the rest call to me from the basement,
marinating in her Chanel No. 5.

"Watch Out for the Old Cows"
—*for Dee*

That's what the ranch foreman said—
when they get old they get mean.

When you herd old cows,
you're supposed to keep your horse away
from their heads, not push them hard.
Herefords have curved, sharp horns
that can unseam you from groin to heart.

Watch out for the old cows—
don't interrupt me when I'm eating,
don't tell me how to do things
I've done for decades, like
drive or think or cook a stew.

My husband keeps a careful distance
in case the horns take a wide sweep
as I'm shaking off the latest invasion
in my space by some political crime,
some machine that breaks when I touch it,
some unforgiveable memory lapse I have to claim.

Everything hurts, but I try to ignore it.
My left psoas muscle, what even is that?

Asymmetries

I have to return to the clinic for more imaging—
they found some "asymmetries."

Nothing is symmetrical in nature,
no two things alike,

but these asymmetries might be fatal—
in nature but unnatural,

like the huge white pines at the end of my driveway
planted together:

one grew stocky and healthy while the other got tall,
started to die, broke in half.

One bird lifts its head higher
in the nest,

grows faster, tips into flight sooner—
if the others even live.

I'm driving on a highway and forget
where I'm going,

as if there's a branch in my brain that split off,
a gap that opened up.

Dear Heart

For decades, I've vibrated to your flutter,
       your arrhythmic tympani.
Every day I worry.
          (wishing will not make us well)

      My Greek cardiologist quotes Homer,
commands me to live without fear,
         then implants a monitor in my breast.

      I can't see it, but I can feel it—
            (wishing will not make us well)
       a short metal warning under the skin,
clocking your syncopated beats.

      My friend's husband, fit in body and mind,
         died at sixty of a massive heart attack.
"Wait—" he said to her.

Jones Beach, Summer 2016

Just dip your toe in
and the ocean grabs your heel
and your hull, staves your keel.
It finds your fingers,

fastens to your flesh, fans out—
as when you lusted after that boy,
or ran away for a day at ten,
or smoked cigars like a man.
The things you have done

that you ought not to have done—
stealing from a locker,
sex play with your sister
on the sprung sofa in Oyster Bay.
Seaweed drags at your waist,

wants you to stop all this forever,
do nothing but drift because
to yearn is to move
and to move is to inflict.

When the tips of your toes touch
the sand below,
it billows into spires
of hottest desires—
blew your first marriage.

You swerved toward someone else,
had to have him even as you knew
it would all soon cool.

Look!—that wild green sea
of life and too much life
that you have to turn
and turn and turn from.

Pulled Back

you crouch and your back seizes
just as the President withdraws
from the Paris climate accord

it's agony to stand upright
the radio says the States
will be going it alone for now

don't lie down keep moving
even if just a little bit and take
whatever you can against the pain

meanwhile things get hotter
sudden fires ash whole towns
moose die starved by a thousand ticks

suddenly you can't move at all
the President has offered
money to strangers for dirt

you're trapped in your house
with its red and gold carpet of leaves
nothing to do about the shakedown

low-lying streets flood everywhere
and we must all bear calmly
the latest contagion

just slide gently through the day
pray for rain to cool the burn
shooting up your spine

black locust trees sway
their tops unleaving too quickly
dry trunks snapping in wind

Half the World

I know where I am
but not all the roads I took to get here
right now Provincetown
watery sky just getting light
shapes in the room returning
I've been up for hours

two trees across the street
sway in a strong wind
pushed together then apart
branches waving branches wavering
like people talking
heads together then not
cropped in cropped out

I remember to visit friends for dinner
forget to bring the dish I promised
forget to apologize
I remember to take my pills
but not what they're called
the names cropped out

I think of my friend
which of her cats died last year
Agnes or Phoebe I knew those cats

half the world's gone missing
I write the names of my pills
put the paper in my wallet

Spring Snow

snow falls straight down
though earth spins
1,000 miles an hour
we're standing on it
but we can't feel it

April 18th too late for a storm
and we've been stuck
inside for weeks
children far away

what if earth stopped
would snow blow to the side
would goldfinches stop brightening
water stop running

would we fall toward the sun
our last moments terror
as all our wars
ceased to matter

I've seen birds crash
against plate glass
and fall dazed

as if an invisible force
struck them down
their own wings providing the speed

In the Fourth Month of the Pandemic

up comes the huge tufted head
cocked to the side
she seems to stare at me
from the top of the pine tree
round yellow eyes with thick brows
broad honey-colored chest

eases out a wing
ducks her head under
rhythmically cleaning

I want to stay until dusk
watch her lethal silent
descent on prey
in the field next door

everything must
still look okay
through her eyes
small me far below
pulling up my mask
in the carless street

Riddles

What blocks breathing to protect breath?
What might leave a three-day residue on a table?
When do uncounted debts become unpayable?
When am I close enough to death?

How does fear attach itself to my hands, my feet?
Why is the doctor's office more dangerous than home?
How is heroism staying indoors alone?
When do airplanes become obsolete?

When do exhalations almost become visible?
When can I hear only my voice in a choir?
Why is the beach forbidden when most desired?
Why must I learn to flee the invisible?

Where does boredom cross paths with dread?
When is my lover contagion instead?

Singing Machine

the dogs are quiet
every cough might be the beginning

for a moment when I wake up
I think in the old way

that I could go shopping
but of course the Mall is empty

Tish said she never worries
about anything

we were teleconferencing about wisdom
her face in extreme close-up

I can still talk to my friends she said
blurring before the lens

that night I recorded my alto part
alone into my phone

timing my wavery voice to match
the click-track of the choir director

peace I leave with you O river
let not your heart be troubled

Without Outside

rain is banging the skylights
outside are beauty and contagion

across the street the field
blooms with scilla deep deep blue

I type with raw clean fingers
and think of my absent children

how can I live without them
how can they live without outside

do I have a regulation mask
can I alone make a wheel or fire

must I sew something amazing
some monster face I wear quietly

this is the long haul
we must be patient and kind

a friend who lives alone asked
when will anyone I love touch me

the news says the earth has stopped shaking
since all our machines have stilled

what do the birds do
when it rains like this

Plague Reunion

her voice a violin
hair a candle
something fierce
something small and air
brandishing a pencil

Emma's come home
middle of the night
with her little dog
old stars stir
spark the big wind

as systems broke
she left her tropical isle
took a plane in mask
and swim goggles
dog at her feet

dark drive home
in a sanitized rental
freezing air conditioning
speeders all around
cutting her off

when she stood
at the foot of the stairs
our feet crept forward
but our heads hung back
we couldn't hug her

shucking her shoes
she arrived cheerful
headed for bed
her dog Hazy waving
his white flag

Processor

My processor is stuck.
I need tea. I want a human
on the other end of the phone,
not some asphalt envelope voice
that says I'm a vegetable.

Did I have breakfast?
Did I have surgery?
The leaves are talking about melancholy,
dreaming near a limestone lake.

My vegetable mind is dangling—
I'm never getting a human on the phone:
human, phone,
breakfast, surgery,

my processor is stuck on the teapot.
There is no tea,
there has never been tea,
just something hot, and I want it now.

ACKNOWLEDGMENTS

Thank you very much to the editors of the magazines and journals which published poems from this collection, sometimes in different forms:

Compose, Dialogist, Gravel, Hawaii Pacific Review, I-70 Review, Ibbetson Street, Indolent Books' *What Rough Beast, The Missouri Review, Naugatuck River Review, New Orleans Review, Ocean State Review, Off the Coast, Paterson Literary Review, Poet Lore, The Poetry Porch, Salamander, Slipstream, South Florida Poetry Journal, Third Wednesday,* and *WomenArts Quarterly.*

Special debts of gratitude to Alan Shapiro, Dorothy Q. Thomas, and Jennifer Clarvoe, for their creativity and generosity looking at early versions, more than once. And to Robert Carr, Christine Casson, Susan Goodman, Daniel Johnson, Dorian Kotsiopoulos, Vicki Murray, and Emily Wheeler, thank you for your perseverance in reading and responding with unfailing insight.

Thanks to my friends, especially Dee Clarke, Parkman and Melinda Howe, Gail Mazur, Mary McClean, Morgan Mead, and Elisabeth Sackton. Gratitude to my family, especially Augusta Read Thomas, Eleanor Thomas, Tony Siesfeld, Emma Siesfeld, Manuel Acuna, Claire Siesfeld, and David Runge, for decades of support, with fun mixed in.

And finally, my gratitude to the generous, creative spirits at
Four Way Books, including Ryan Murphy, Clarissa Long,
Colin Bonini, Hannah Matheson, and peerless editor Sally Ball.
Deepest thanks to publisher Martha Rhodes for bringing this book
into being.

Cammy Thomas' first book, *Cathedral of Wish*, received the Norma Farber First Book Award from the Poetry Society of America. A fellowship from the Ragdale Foundation helped her complete her second, *Inscriptions*. Both were published by Four Way Books. Her poems have appeared in numerous journals, and in *Poems in the Aftermath*, an anthology. Two of her poems under the title *Far Past War* are the text for a choral work by her sister, composer Augusta Read Thomas. *Far Past War* premieres at the National Cathedral in Washington, DC, in 2022. She taught college and high school English and creative writing for many years, and now teaches ancient and Renaissance texts to adults. She lives in Massachusetts. For more information, visit cammythomas.com.

Publication of this book was made possible by grants and donations. We are also grateful to those individuals who participated in our 2020 Build a Book Program. They are:

Anonymous (14), Robert Abrams, Nancy Allen, Maggie Anderson, Sally Ball, Matt Bell, Laurel Blossom, Adam Bohannon, Lee Briccetti, Therese Broderick, Jane Martha Brox, Christopher Bursk, Liam Callanan, Anthony Cappo, Carla & Steven Carlson, Paul & Brandy Carlson, Renee Carlson, Cyrus Cassells, Robin Rosen Chang, Jaye Chen, Edward W. Clark, Andrea Cohen, Ellen Cosgrove, Peter Coyote, Janet S. Crossen, Kim & David Daniels, Brian Komei Dempster, Matthew DeNichilo, Carl Dennis, Patrick Donnelly, Charles Douthat, Morgan Driscoll, Lynn Emanuel, Monica Ferrell, Elliot Figman, Laura Fjeld, Michael Foran, Jennifer Franklin, Sarah Freligh, Helen Fremont & Donna Thagard, Reginald Gibbons, Jean & Jay Glassman, Ginny Gordon, Lauri Grossman, Naomi Guttman & Jonathan Mead, Mark Halliday, Beth Harrison, Jeffrey Harrison, Page Hill Starzinger, Deming Holleran, Joan Houlihan, Thomas & Autumn Howard, Elizabeth Jackson, Christopher Johanson, Voki Kalfayan, Maeve Kinkead, David Lee, Jen Levitt, Howard Levy, Owen Lewis, Jennifer Litt, Sara London & Dean Albarelli, David Long, James Longenbach, Excelsior Love, Ralph & Mary Ann Lowen, Jacquelyn Malone, Donna Masini, Catherine McArthur, Nathan McClain, Richard McCormick, Victoria McCoy, Ellen McCulloch-Lovell, Judith McGrath, Debbie & Steve Modzelewski, Rajiv Mohabir, James T. F. Moore, Beth Morris, John Murillo & Nicole Sealey, Michael & Nancy Murphy, Maria Nazos, Kimberly Nunes, Bill O'Brien, Susan Okie & Walter Weiss, Rebecca Okrent, Sam Perkins, Megan Pinto, Kyle Potvin, Glen Pourciau, Kevin Prufer, Barbara Ras, Victoria Redel, Martha Rhodes, Paula Rhodes, Paula Ristuccia, George & Nancy Rosenfeld, M. L. Samios, Peter & Jill Schireson, Rob Schlegel, Roni & Richard Schotter, Jane Scovell, Andrew Seligsohn & Martina Anderson, James & Nancy Shalek, Soraya Shalforoosh, Peggy Shinner, Dara-Lyn Shrager, Joan Silber, Emily Sinclair, James Snyder & Krista Fragos, Alice St. Claire-Long, Megan Staffel, Bonnie Stetson, Yerra Sugarman, Dorothy Tapper Goldman, Marjorie & Lew Tesser, Earl Teteak, Parker & Phyllis Towle, Pauline Uchmanowicz, Rosalynde Vas Dias, Connie Voisine, Valerie Wallace, Doris Warriner, Ellen Doré Watson, Martha Webster & Robert Fuentes, Calvin Wei, Bill Wenthe, Allison Benis White, Michelle Whittaker, and Ira Zapin.